Chief Sitting Bull

by Alan E. Grey
Illustrations by Dwane Cude

Chief Sitting Bull

For information address: Northwest Publishing, Inc.
6906 South 300 West, Salt Lake City, Utah 84047

First Printing 1994

ISBN: 1-56901-427-2

NPI books are published by Northwest Publishing, Incorporated,
6906 South 300 West, Salt Lake City, Utah 84047.
The Name "NPI" and the "NPI" logo are trademarks belonging to
Northwest Publishing, Incorporated.

Printed in the United States of America.
10 9 8 7 6 5 4 3 2 1

Chief Sitting Bull

The story I tell you

I know it is true,

For I am Sitting Bull,

Chief of the Sioux.

My people were free

To travel and roam.

The sky was their heaven,

The earth was their home.

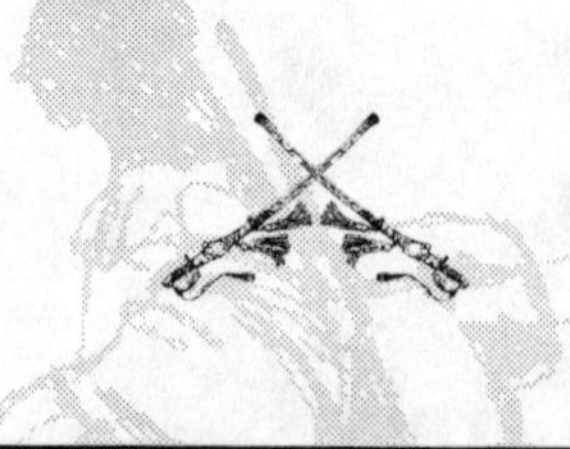

We lived off the land

Like my people before,

We took what we needed,

And asked for no more.

Now in the spring,

After winter's deep snow,

My people were hunting

The Great Buffalo.

For days we had traveled,

Each day to the West.

The women and children

All needed a rest.

We looked for a camp
That we could defend,
And found such a place
At a small river bend.

We made our camp

That late June morn

At a bend of a river,

The Little Bighorn.

My people were safe,

They camped without fear,

Since warriors were scouting

The land far and near.

And from these scouts

We learned one day,

That troops of the White Man

Were coming our way.

13

The White Man's Chief
They told me was there,
The one they called Custer,
With long flowing hair.

I told all my scouts

To keep them in sight,

To watch every movement

All day and all night.

For I, Sitting Bull,

Just wanted to know

What they were doing

And where they might go.

We watched General Custer

Divide up his troops,

Then fit them for battle

In three equal groups.

The first of the groups

Got their horses to ride,

Then forded the river

To the western side.

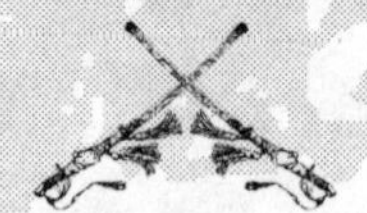

They made a large circle

With full battle gear,

Approaching our camp

From the west, or the rear.

Then Custer came riding,
He'd waited till then
To ride toward our camp
With two hundred men.

My people were ready,

My warriors were fit;

If a battle they wanted,

A battle they'd get.

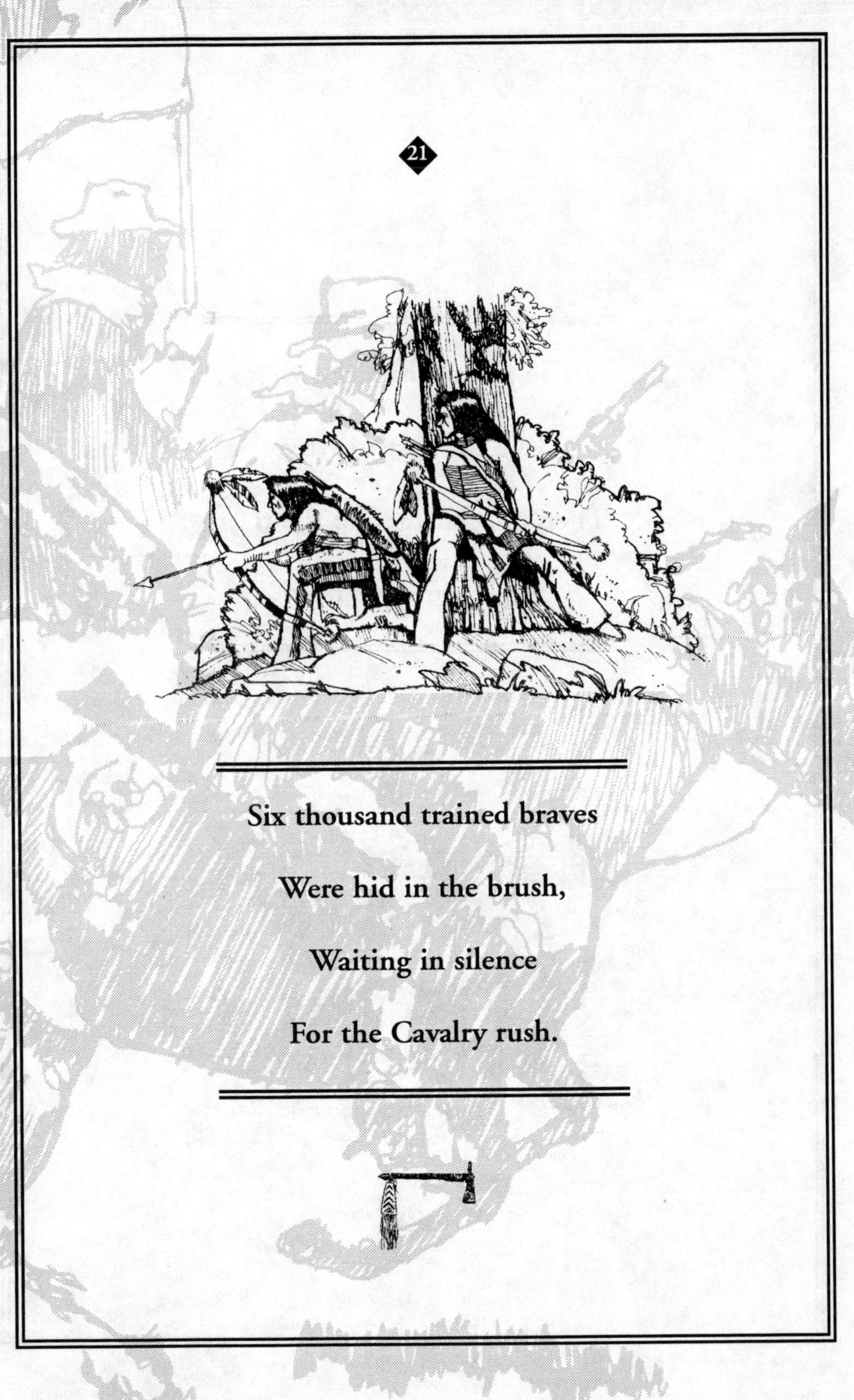

Six thousand trained braves

Were hid in the brush,

Waiting in silence

For the Cavalry rush.

The troops from the West

Were the first to arrive;

Then they charged to the river

In columns of five.

When they started to cross

The small river banks,

My braves began shooting

Right into their ranks.

When they started to turn,
We cut their retreat,
So they scattered and ran
In utter defeat.

After the battle,
We looked all around,
And found fifty troopers
Out there on the ground.

We took new positions,
With just time to hide,
When Custer rode in
From the eastern side.

Their banners were flying
Both bright and large,
And the bugler in front
Was sounding the charge.

The troops into battle
By Custer were led,
His long golden saber
Held over his head.

While Custer and troops

Raced over the ground,

We lay there in ambush,

Not making a sound.

Above all the roar

Of the horses' beat,

We gave a war whoop,

And jumped to our feet.

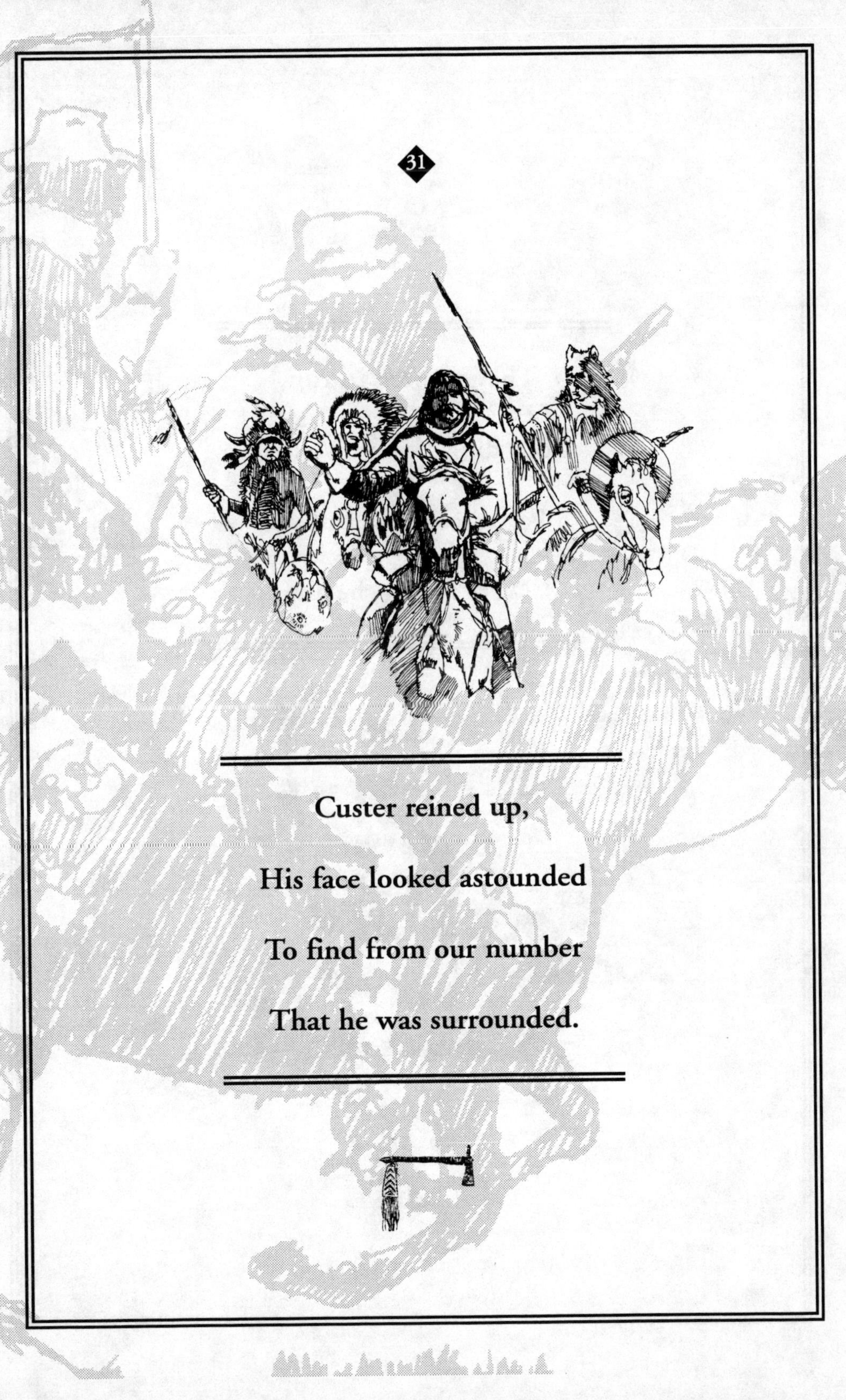

Custer reined up,
His face looked astounded
To find from our number
That he was surrounded.

They wanted to run,

But didn't know where,

For arrows and bullets

Were filling the air.

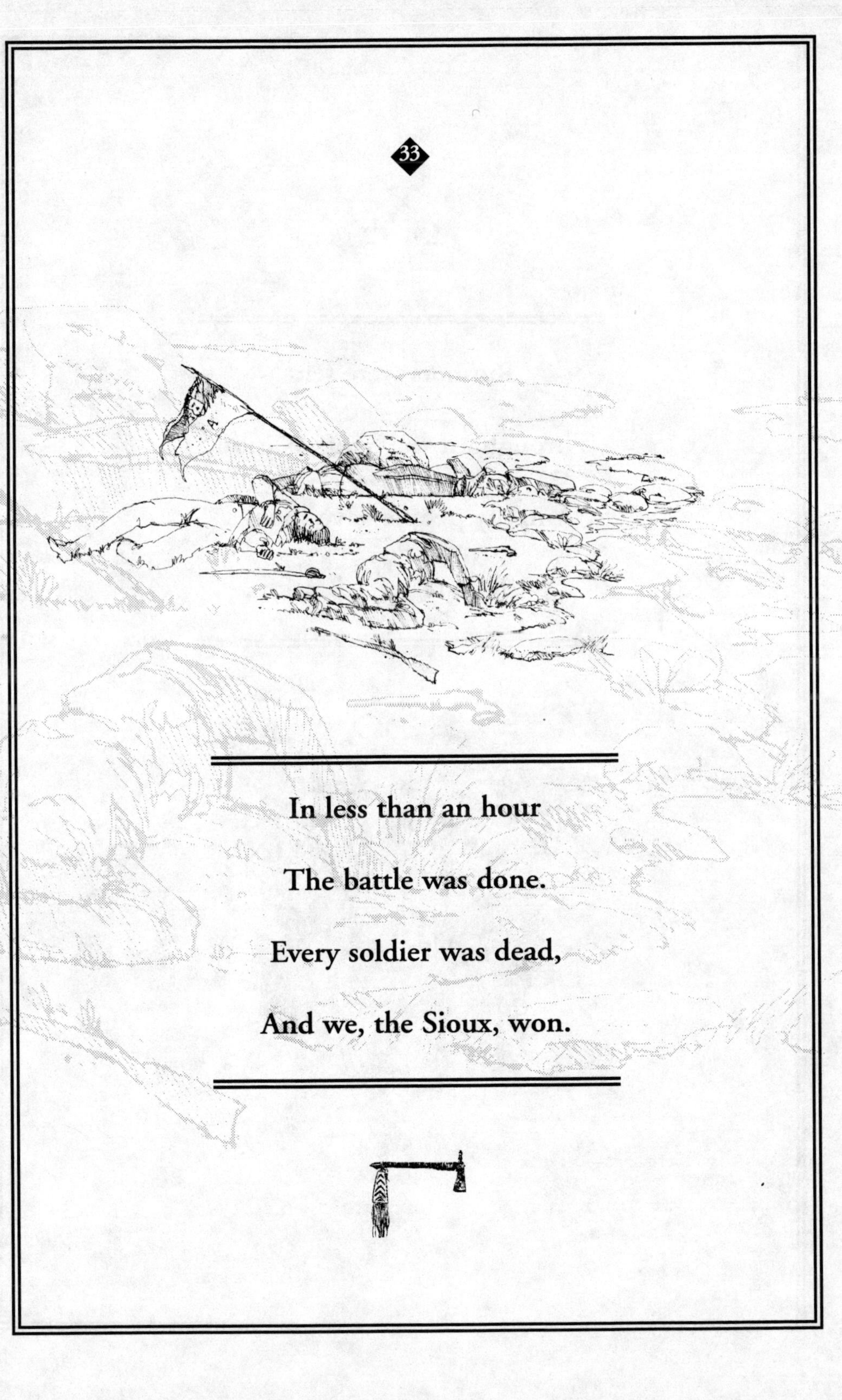

In less than an hour
The battle was done.
Every soldier was dead,
And we, the Sioux, won.

Runners were sent

Throughout the Sioux Nation,

And my people gave thanks

With a great celebration.

We still didn't know

Why the troops came along;

We'd broken no treaty,

We'd done nothing wrong.

They give us some land

And say we must stay,

Then send in their troops

To take it away.

Now many moons later,

Our hopes are no more.

We'd won a great battle,

And then lost the war.